# Seeing and Hearing Well

## by Robin Nelson

Series consultants: Sonja Green, MD, and
Distinguished Professor Emerita Ann Nolte, PhD

Lerner Books • London • New York • Minneapolis

This book was first published in the United States of America in 2006.

First published in the United Kingdom in 2008 by
Lerner Books,
Dalton House,
60 Windsor Avenue,
London SW19 2RR

Website address: www.lernerbooks.co.uk

This edition was updated and edited for UK publication by Discovery Books Ltd., Unit 3, 37 Watling Street, Leintwardine, Shropshire SY7 0LW

Words in **bold** type are explained in the glossary on page 31.

British Library Cataloguing in Publication Data

Nelson, Robin, 1971-
  Seeing and hearing well. - (Pull ahead books. Health)
  1. Visual acuity - Juvenile literature 2. Hearing -
  Juvenile literature
  I. Title
  612.8'4

ISBN-13: 978 1 58013 403 3

Printed in China

Look around.  What can you see? Now
close your eyes.  What can you hear?

Seeing and hearing are two of our **senses.** We use our senses to learn about the world around us.

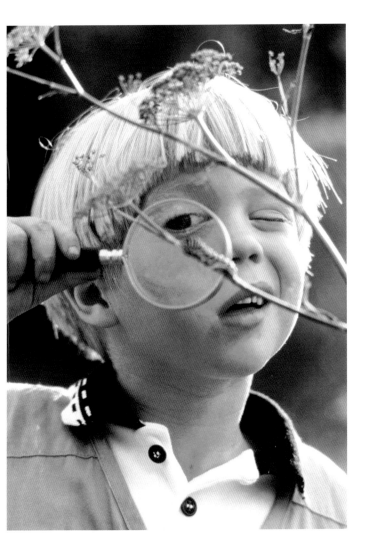

Eyes let us see everything around us. We can see a friend or a tiny insect. We can see words in a book.

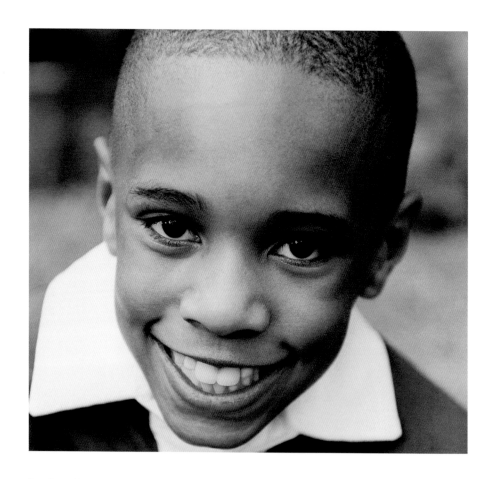

It is important to keep our eyes healthy.
How can we take care of our eyes?

Wear safety glasses or goggles. They protect our eyes when playing some sports.

Wear sunglasses on sunny days. Sunglasses protect your eyes from bright sunlight. And never look directly at the sun! It can burn your eyes.

If it feels like you have something in your eye, ask an adult for help.

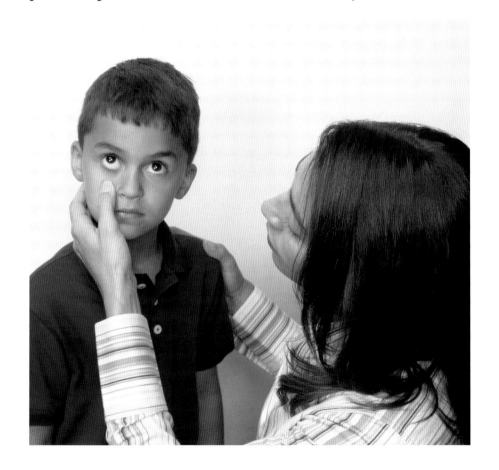

Sit near a bright light when you read. Reading in the dark makes your eyes work too hard.

Your eyes
get tired if
you watch
television or
use computers
a lot.  Give
your eyes a
break and do
something
new.

Keep sharp objects, like scissors or
pencils, away from your eyes.

Eat foods like
carrots,
dark green
vegetables
and oranges.
They are
good for
your eyes.

Sometimes people need to wear **glasses** to help them see. You might need glasses if the words in a book look blurry.

You might also need glasses if things far away look blurry. Tell your teacher or a parent if you can't read the words on the board at school.

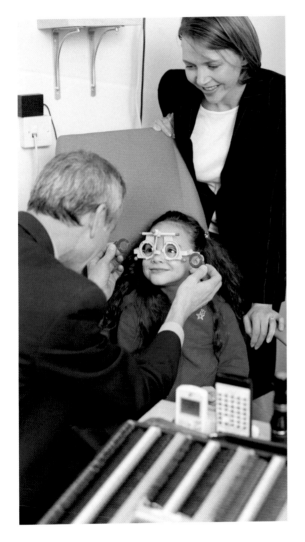

You will visit an eye doctor if you have trouble seeing. An eye doctor is called an **optician.** A doctor who can do eye surgery is called an **ophthalmologist**.

An optitian has tools to test how well your eyes work.  Your optician will tell you if you need to wear glasses.

Hearing is an important sense too. We hear with our ears. How can you keep your ears healthy?

Keep the outside of your ears clean. But never poke anything inside your ear! Not even a **cotton bud**! You could hurt your ear.

Too much loud noise is bad for your hearing.  Loud noises can make your ears ring and feel blocked.

Your music is too loud if someone next to you can hear the music coming from your headphones. It might **damage** your ears.

# Turn down the **volume**!

What should you do if you are close to a noisy machine? You can wear **earmuffs** or earplugs to protect your hearing.

See a doctor if your ears hurt or feel blocked. The doctor will look in your ears with a special torch.

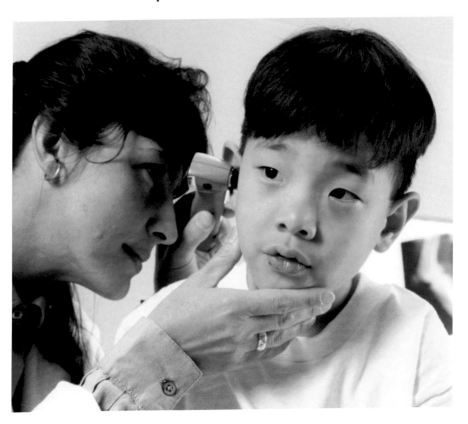

Doctors and schools give hearing tests. These tests make sure your ears are working well.

Doctors and schools also check your
eyes.  This is called an eye test.

It is important to keep our eyes and ears healthy. If we take care of them, we will be seeing and hearing well for a lifetime!

# Doctor Visits

Your doctor checks your eyes and ears to make sure they are working well. You may see a special doctor if you have trouble seeing or hearing.

## What happens at a hearing test?

■ The doctor will look in your ear with an otoscope. This tool lets the doctor see all the tiny parts inside your ear.

■ You will wear big headphones for a hearing test.

■ Sounds will be played in the headphones. You will need to make a signal, like raising your hand, every time you hear a sound.

# What happens at an eye test?

■ The doctor will look in your eyes with a light. The doctor will shine the light as you look up, down, left and right.

■ You will read from an eye chart. This chart has letters in many different sizes. This test measures how well you can see from far away.

■ You will cover one eye and read the chart. Read until the letters are too small or too blurry to read. Then cover the other eye and read the chart again.

■ You will read some words up close. This test will measure how well you see close to you.

# Books and Websites

## Books

Llewellyn, Claire. *Sound and Hearing* (Start-Up Science) Evans Brothers Ltd, 2004.

Mackill, Mary. *Seeing* (Read and Learn: Super Senses) Raintree Publishers, 2007.

Royston, Angela. *Healthy Eyes and Ears* (Look After Yourself) Heinemann, 2003.

Royston, Angela. *Sound and Hearing* (My World of Science) Heinemann, 2002.

Spilsbury, Louise. *Why Should I Turn Down the Volume?: And Other Questions About Healthy Ears and Eyes* (Body Matters) Heinemann, 2003.

## Websites

*Juniors first for health - Great Ormond Street Hospital*
   http://www.childrenfirst.nhs.uk/juniors/body/eyes.html
   http://www.childrenfirst.nhs.uk/juniors/body/ears.html

*NHS - Your Body*
   http://www.suttonandmerton.nhs.uk/ec/funforkids/update/readn ew.asp?id=4#eyesandears

# Glossary

**cotton bud:** a stick with cotton wool on both ends used to clean the outsides of ears

**damage:** hurt, harm

**earmuffs:** a covering worn over the ears

**glasses:** a frame with lenses that you wear on your face to help your eyes see better

**ophthalmologist:** a doctor who can do eye surgery

**optician:** an eye doctor

**senses:** the five ways our bodies get information.  The five senses are hearing, seeing, smelling, tasting and touching.

**volume:** the loudness of a sound

# Index

**Photo Acknowledgements**

The photographs in this book appear with the permission of: © Joe Gemignani photography, cover; © Andy King, p 3; © age fotostock/SuperStock, pp 4, 24, 27; © Ariel Skelley/CORBIS, p 5; Digital Vision Royalty Free, pp 6, 21; © Bob Winsett/CORBIS, p 7; EyeWire by Getty Images, p 8; © Todd Strand/Independent Picture Service, pp 9, 13, 18, 19, 22; © Chris Fairclough/Discovery Picure Library, p 10; © Royalty-Free/CORBIS, pp 11, 12, 17; © Jose Luis Pelaez, Inc./CORBIS, p 14; © Heide Benser/zefa/CORBIS, p 15; BananaStock Ltd., p 16; © Kwame Zikomo/SuperStock, p 20; © Tom Stewart/zefa/CORBIS, p 23; © Sam Lund/Independent Picture Service, p 25; © PhotoDisc Royalty Free by Getty Images, pp 26, 29.